I0485014

This business module is dedicated to all the ambitious, hard-working individuals
that strive for a prosperous way of life.
- Mark J. Allen

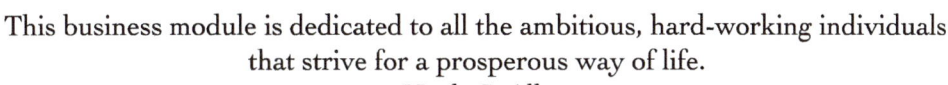

"Never give in, never give in, never; never; never; never!"
- Winston Churchill's „Never Give In" Speech of 1941

Contents

Part One

Get the business started

Part Two

Get the business

Congratulations on your new investment!

You've just taken your first step towards becoming your own boss. A day wasted means less money in your pocket, so let's get started right away...

It might seem like a bad idea to start your own business when people around you are losing theirs, but as long as you know what you're doing, you have the right set of tools to get the job done and you have confidence in your ability to provide a service that is better than your competitors, you can get out there and start earning a decent living, and in time, build a profitable and rewarding business.

So how do you do it?
You start small and you think BIG...

Our common-sense, easy-to-apply, step-by-step guides to starting your own business are the quickest and easiest way to become fully operational.

We don't teach you how to be an auctioneer... but we do offer you the best advice on how to get your new business up and running... starting today!

Auctioneering Business Start-Up Guide

What your guide contains...

// Forming legal ownership of your business
// Securing adequate insurance protection and business licenses
// Applying for a small business loan
// Establishing an effective website as your storefront
// Designing business cards that send the right message
// Selecting and securing your equipment
// Choosing uniforms and customizing company letterhead
// 5 cost effective ways of promoting your business

Follow our fail proof marketing techniques for guaranteed success with your business!

Know how to land the most rewarding opportunities, grow your business and satisfy your customers. We'll show you how to cultivate word of mouth buzz about your services and gain lucrative commercial contracts!

Join the top associations for increased business referrals. Learn which business and trade memberships are worthwhile and how you can best 'work' the system!

Get the best advice for your advertising dollar. Don't waste any of your money on ineffective, expensive advertising. Use the most powerful and low cost marketing methods in the business to make your phone ring!

Cultivate commercial business for a lifetime of success. Follow the rainbow of commercial and government contracts to a pot of gold. Learn the quickest way to gain repeat business and keep your customers happy.

Freebies, Freebies, Freebies! Find out which acts of goodwill shall return your favors tenfold! Why you should give and what you can receive in return...

Forming legal ownership

// First decide how you want to set up ownership of your business for tax and liability purposes. There are four basic types of business: Sole Proprietorship, Limited Liability Company, General Partnership and C Corporation.

A sole proprietorship has no separate existence from its owner. The person who sets up the company has responsibility for the debts of the company. A sole proprietor may do business under his/her own name or under a trade name, and in most US states, you will be required to register your trade name with a government agency, allowing you to open a business account at a bank.

A limited liability company (LLC) is a business that provides limited liability to its owners. An LLC has certain characteristics of both a corporation and a partnership. It is often more flexible than a corporation and it is well-suited for companies with a single owner.

A general partnership refers to a business association or an unincorporated company formed by two or more people who are personally liable for any legal action and/or debts the company may face. All partners share equally in responsibility and liability.

A c corporation (INC or LTD) is a business that is separate from the person who formed it. In the US, most major companies and many smaller ones are treated as c corporations for federal income tax purposes.

// Talk to an accountant and they'll help you decide the most appropriate type of ownership for your business aspirations. If you're planning to start as a one man show, a sole proprietorship is the best option for you.

// As your business grows, you may decide to incorporate your company to protect and separate your personal assets from your business assets. Discuss this matter with an accountant or lawyer on how to go about this.

Choosing a business name that clearly communicates what you do

// Make an impression with your company name. To help people identify and locate you, the name you select should include some reference to your business.

// If using a name other than your personal name, you must file for a fictitious name registration when you apply for your business license and open a business bank account. Go to the US Small Business Administration website at www.sba.gov for more information about this.

// You will also need a dedicated business phone line, separate from your personal phone and preferably for a mobile or cell phone so that you can receive calls and leave voice messages while on job sites. As an auctioneer, you will more than likely be taking calls while on the run!

Applying for a business license

// Business licenses are permits issued by government agencies that allow you or your company to conduct business within a specific jurisdiction, e.g. the state of Florida. Business licenses vary between countries, states and local municipalities. There are often many licenses, registrations and certifications required to conduct a business in a single location, so make sure you check with your local government to find out what is required to get you up and running.

// Business registration, separate from your license, may also be required. The type of business you own, as well as your physical location (address) will determine your license requirement. Other determining factors may include the number of employees you have working for you, as well as the type of business ownership, e.g. sole proprietorship or general partnership. Government agencies can fine or close a business that is operating without the required licenses and registration – so make sure you have your paperwork in order.

// To operate in most counties and states of the US, you'll be required to carry your license with you at all times. Check with your local city hall for instructions. Your business will likely need a yearly occupational license check with your county office which will cost you around $100 annually. As laws differ by state, ask your local licensing office about your county's requirements for legal operating rules and regulations.

Securing adequate insurance protection

// It is crucial that you do not start running your business without insurance coverage. In the event of an accident and without proper protection, you will find yourself out of a job (or worse still, in the midst of a lawsuit) no sooner than you started. Talk to your local insurer about the best type of protection for your operation as there are a number of different business insurance policies available.

// The most common business liability insurance provides one million dollars worth of cover, varying by agency and state, and costing you around $1,000 annually. This sounds like a lot of money to pay upfront, however beyond protecting your customers' property from possible damage, a typical general liability insurance policy will also cover customer injury, personal injury and advertising injury claims. Professional liability provides even greater coverage for your business – including claims about negligence, misrepresentation, violation of good faith and fair dealing, and inaccurate advice.

// Most commercial businesses such as retail outlets and restaurants will not employ you unless you can show them proof of insurance and/or workers compensation insurance. As a sole business owner, you can file yourself as exempt from workers compensation policy, saving yourself a bundle of annual dues.

// However, if you employ people to work for you, you should familiarize yourself with this type of insurance in case of a workplace accident or negligence caused or suffered by your employees.

Financing your operation

// Small business loans aim to help qualified businesses obtain financing when they might not be eligible for funding through normal lending channels. Go to the US Small Business Administration (SBA) website: www.sba.gov for more information about the different types of loans and grants available and how you can apply.

// It is important to note that your loan may still be granted by commercial and private lending institutions like banks, however, a government body like the SBA will act as a guarantor for your loan. Make sure you seek as much advice as possible when deciding on how to finance your new venture. Speak to other small business owners or people you know how have secured loans in the past, and read the terms and conditions of your repayments carefully.

Establishing an effective website as your storefront

// Without a retail outlet or storefront you must have a website, but very few auctioneers do. Why is this so important? Websites boost sales, increase customer satisfaction, improve overall perception of the quality of your business, enhance your company's image, test and expand markets, and reduce operational costs. It's the 21 century - you must get with the program!

// Your webpage can help make or break sales. Remember that appearance says it all. Unless you're good at web design and layout, plan to pay someone $100-$500 to design your site for you. Students can often design effective websites at a fraction of the cost. An appealing, professional looking site tells prospective customers they can trust you to provide an exceptional service. Make sure your information is easy to read, user friendly and includes everything your customers need to know about you - such as your contact details, the type of work you do,
and some client testimonials.

// Many business professionals, especially realtors, communicate via the internet and as well as your cell phone number, you must provide an email address to your customers. You don't want to miss out on jobs because potential clients could not get in contact with you easily. Your website is your storefront and could be a deal maker or breaker so be sure to spend time updating it and keeping the information current.

Designing business cards

// When you're brand new in the business of auctioneering, business cards are a relatively cheap and incredibly effective way of advertising your services. Get your cards printed after you have established your business name, contact telephone number, web address, email, license, and insurance. Make sure all details are correct and not likely to change. Check local printers for prices, which range from $50 to $150 per thousand cards.

// Again, appearance is the key, especially for a mobile business with no storefront. Choosing good quality paper might mean having to spend a little extra on your business cards, but this will build customer confidence in your service from the beginning. It's a good idea to distribute at least half of your business cards in your first month of operation – either by handing them out to people you meet or by doing a letterbox drop in your area. Hand out more than one card to let people know that you welcome referrals.

Selecting and securing your equipment

// Now that your paperwork is in order, it's time for the exciting part, purchasing the equipment you will need for your business.

// Speak to an accountant about purchasing a car for business and how you can claim this expense for tax purposes. It's a good idea to keep a log book of gas, mileage and servicing/repairs.

// Your vehicle should be reliable and clean at all times. Select a spacious vehicle with a large trunk — it is by far the simplest way to load and unload your equipment. A plain color such as white or silver will allow you to display a large promotional magnet or a wrap-around banner for advertising purposes.

// Classified ads or local used car dealers offer great deals on vehicles that are only a few years old. Get a couple of quotes from different insurance providers – and make sure the insurance policy covers all of your equipment as well as your vehicle. Ensure your equipment is fully secured whenever you are out on the road.

Purchasing wisely

// Before you go on a spending spree you must create a budget, allocate how much you can afford to spend on the tools of your trade, and stick to it! Remember that almost all of your startup costs relate to your business equipment – so make a list of everything you need. Be frugal with your purchases, but don't be tempted to buy cheap or second-hand equipment with no warranty. As an auctioneer, the most important piece of equipment besides your voice and your sales ability is your sound system. 'Technical difficulties' will not win you repeat business.

// So long as you can afford to make payments, open a credit account at one of the major electronic stores. Credit plans are fairly relaxed and your credit rating doesn't have to be perfect to apply. With a credit account, you can purchase almost everything you need with low monthly repayments. Take advantage of interest free offers if available. Given the current credit crisis, it is not wise to add to your debts and purchase items that you can not afford. Stick to your budget and build up your equipment over time, once you start making money from your business.

Sample budget:

Annual business expenses

Business license	$	100
General liability insurance	$	1,000
Motor insurance	$	500
Equipment insurance	$	100
Travel expenses	$	2,000
Loan repayments	$	2,000
Postage	$	100
Total	**$**	**5,800**

Startup expenses

Microphone	$	100
Amp	$	100
Customized cap	$	40
Second-hand vehicle	$	5,000
Business cards	$	150
Letterhead	$	150
Total	**$**	**5,540**

Keeping your uniforms, hats and customized paperwork simple

// Check your local mall or Yellow Pages for promotional companies who can design and/or imprint your logo on to customized uniforms and hats. Don't go overboard. You do not need to be dressed from head to toe in your company colors!

// You may wish to design your own company logo by using business or design software. Business startup kits are handy for do-it-yourself stationery. Remember something that looks professional will impress your customers, while a sloppy quotation or receipt may deter them from using your service again. If you don't have the creative know-how to produce your own paperwork, printing companies offer package deals on receipts, quotation sheets, inventory lists, letterhead, envelopes and other forms you'll need to run your business smoothly. Make sure it looks good and is easy to read.

// Now that you've got the basics to get you started, it's time to start talking like an auctioneer!

Researching your product and getting the best advice from the experts

// Make sure you research your product and your marketplace. Even if you have some auctioneering experience, you will still need to read up on the latest information on sales, advertising and the property market. If you can't afford to attend a real estate course, find some reading material online or from your local library, or call in to the nearest estate agent and ask to speak to one of the auctioneers. Explain that you are new to the business and would like to know if there are any books or training tools recommended by the experts.

// Go along to live auctions and take notes on what the auctioneer says and does. The majority of your business will come from local homeowners and businesses so focus on them – get an understanding of what they want and what they expect.

// Unless you're experienced in the art of the auction chant, you must practice and master the technique. You should be warming up your voice 30 minutes prior to any event. Practice tongue twisters and counting exercises for an hour a day. Work as a ringman at auctions until you are 100% confident. Use a strong, positive approach!

Charging your customers

// When starting out, charge 10% buyers or sellers premium or simply price yourself slightly below your competition. You may want to underbid your prices in order to build up your customer base. You can always increase your prices further down the track.

// Mystery shop' your competitors and ask about their going rates. Labor rates differ from community to community (due to economic and market factors) so it's a good idea to check on local information and trends. You may wish to simplify things and charge a standard hourly rate, for instance $50 an hour. Make sure this hourly rate covers your travel costs and what you paid for your advertising and equipment.

// If you have a big job to do and will be working for a customer over a period of days or weeks, keep detailed records of the hours you work (dates and times) and the money you spend on gas and equipment. When it comes time to send them your final invoice, they can not question or dispute your claim if you have documented your work thoroughly.

// Don't underestimate the importance of referral business. As long as your customers are satisfied with your work and find you helpful and easy to deal with, you should be able to boost your sales by word of mouth.

Promoting your business

// To promote your new service and secure business quickly, it is important to apply five essential, cost efficient marketing and communication techniques. If you are providing a valuable service to the community and your customers are satisfied with your work, word of mouth will bring in more business than you can handle.

// People are always buying and selling property so it's important to remind yourself that every home or business can benefit from your service. There are a lot of customers out there. Opportunities are endless. When out driving or walking through your neighborhood, take a look around at all the potential business opportunities and let them inspire you. Jump on the scene with confidence and start working right away.

First, you have to believe in what you do! Second, you have to believe that you can do it better than your competitors!

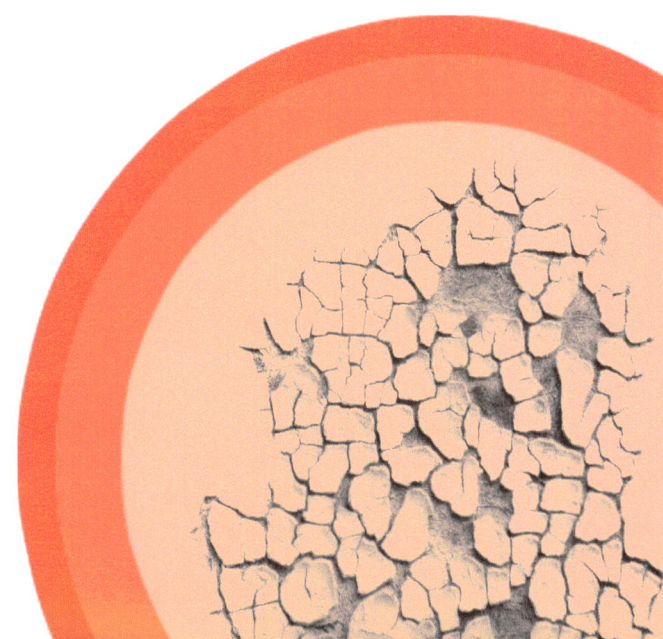

Apply these five cost-effective ways to promote your business and attract new customers:

1. Conducting pinpoint mailing to maximize opportunity.
2. Learning and living by the retention rule.
3. Making friends in the business by joining local associations.
4. Investing wisely in advertising.
5. Giving away freebies and supporting charity organizations.

These marketing techniques are a step in the right direction to assuring your success!

Conducting pinpoint mailing to maximize opportunity

// Here's a way of getting around most home associations' no-soliciting rule... First target wealthy neighborhoods with homes in the $200 thousand range. You will find many of these homes surrounding golf courses. As long as these communities are not gated, drive through the neighborhood and start writing down addresses where you see "for sale" signs.

// Though you may observe just 30 or 40 homes, plan to send these potential customers hand-written cards or letters in hand-written envelopes advertising your services. Unlike bulk or junk mail, hand-written letters aren't thrown away without being opened. People are more likely to open a personal letter or greeting card unlike other "junk mail" that gets automatically trashed.

// Residents' names are free public information. After compiling your address list, go online to a public information website, type the address and zip code into the search engine, and a name will be displayed alongside the address.

// Send your potential customers birthday-sized cards with a message such as: "When it's time to put your house on the market, you can trust our experienced and professional auctioneers to sell at the price you want". Be sure to add your contact details: *Action Auctions, Telephone 888-888-8888, P.S. We are licensed and insured!*

// The key to pinpoint mailing is to personalize your letter so that the customer wants to do business with you. If your penmanship isn't good, pay someone to make your message more readable and give it some significance. Your average cost per card is about $1-2 including postage and it is well worth the money you spend, especially if it lands you a regular contract.

Learning and living by the retention rule

// It's important to understand the 80/20 rule, anticipating that 80% of your business will come from 20% of your customers. Keep in contact with any people you have done business with in the past or customers who have expressed an interest in your services.

// Keeping a record of all customers and jobs performed will form the basis of your marketing database. Three to six months after a job, you should send out hand-written cards or letters reminding customers of your services with a message like: "Time to move on? Need to sell? Call us for advice! Thanks for your continued support!"

// Don't forget holidays or special events, even oddball ones like Groundhog Day or Earth Day. They might present the perfect opportunity for a sale or special offer. People love personal and quirky correspondence and these $2 letters are worth every single penny!

Making friends in the business by joining local associations

// Joining business associations help you to build lots of productive working relationships. Attending conferences and trade shows can also provide the perfect opportunity to network. Associations such as the local Chamber of Commerce, Real Estate Association and Hotel & Condominium Association are absolutely invaluable in terms of referrals and new business opportunities. You should note that these organizations have annual membership fees but once you start talking to the right people and they begin to send business your way, you'll be happy you made the decision to join!

// You'll be surprised that some of these organizations are not widely known and have few members – even in major cities. If you are the only auctioneer in your neighborhood who is a member of an association, you may find yourself with a huge increase in referral rates, making it much easier for you to capture your market.

// Once a member of an association, you should follow three essential rules to maximize your chances of getting referrals:

1. Be visible - A gym membership is worthless if you never go to the gym and so are these association memberships if you don't make the most of them! You must get involved in the group, attend meetings and be available and interested in following up on referrals.

2. Build relationships - Other business professionals must learn to like and trust you before they send business your way. Spend time talking to people about what you do and what they do and learn and understand your trade.

3. Get involved in trade shows and committees - Joining a council or committee within a business association is the best way to get the most from your annual membership dues. Volunteering at a trade show is another way you can make contacts and increase business.

Chamber of Commerce

// Joining the local Chamber of Commerce provides instant access to other local business owners – and it's your chance to contact other people who may partner with you. Start talking to all the property managers, realtors, appraisers, building developers, town planners, home inspectors, painting specialists and other trades people related to your business. Give these companies your promotional material, business cards and any other printed items that explain your service. Request their business cards in return. These people are more likely to recommend your business if you're returning the favor. As they say in the business world: Scratch my back and I'll scratch yours!

// Most Chambers have weekly 'leads group' meetings. Business professionals meet for breakfast, lunch or dinner for the sole purpose of sharing 'leads' with each other. Most groups limit the number to one or two people from each profession, allowing just two realtors, bankers, accountants, etc. to join the group. You'll likely be the only auctioneer in this group. What an excellent opportunity to capture corporate clients such as real estate agents, retail store owners, restaurateurs, and other businesses who are looking to sell their property.

// Retail customers who request auctioneers every couple of years or more regularly are gold! Live by the 80/20 rule! One good contract for routine auctions may give you commission business for your entire year. Even if you don't seal the deal, they may let you quote them just to see if your prices are competitive. Try to underbid their current auctioneer if at all possible – even by as little as $5 an hour. Consider not charging the seller but tack on a 10% buyer's premium.

National Association of Realtors

// It's a good idea to join this local organization as an affiliate member to gain access to marketing, financial services, educational tools and industry information. Within the association, you can also join institutions, societies and councils, giving you the opportunity to network with other professionals.

// Depending on the size of your town and how many locals belong to the realtor association, you may have a couple of hundred agents using your services. Realtors push homeowners to sell quickly. In today's unstable financial climate, properties are being sold more and more via auction due to foreclosures or rapid turnover. This is bad news for the homeowner but great news for you! A good rapport with association members is one of the best ways to stay on top of your business - so be sure to develop and promote a productive working relationship with these colleagues. To find out how to join the association, go the website: www.realtor.org.

National Association of Condo and Hotel Owners

// Just as important as your real estate group is the hotel and condo association. In fact, the majority of hotels and condos are privately owned, which means this group relies heavily on auctioneers when buying and selling their properties, and could prove to be some of your most profitable clients.

// Membership benefits include listing in a business network directory, discount registrations at trade shows and conferences and access to property news and information, research and data. More information is available at: www.nacho.us.

Investing wisely in advertising

// No doubt you are already aware that advertising is an absolute necessity for your business. Before investing in an advertising campaign, ask yourself how much you're willing to spend to secure just one job and whether you'll make a profit after your expenses.

// Your budget dictates how you should spend your dollars. Joining associations and sending hand-written letters to hand-picked clients will help you aggressively draw in business. When it comes to other, more 'passive' types of advertising, it is recommended that you use only the most essential and cost efficient means.

// Remember that once the client has heard about you, they must be able to locate you. If they can't find your details, they'll choose another provider instead – so make sure all of your contact details are up-to-date and widely distributed.

Yellow Pages and other service directories

// Advertising in the Yellow Pages can be expensive, so make sure you check prices before you place an ad. Decide which of the two or three directories floating around town is best for you and your budget. Check out your competitors' ads. If nobody has a display ad, then it might benefit you to be the first one in the book!

// People usually call display ads first, then bold-faced ads, before searching all listings alphabetically from the top down. Designing an ad that will stand out will be worth the money spent. Your ad should state your company name, telephone number, license and insurance numbers as well as your website address.

Pamphlets that enhance your service

// In addition to a business card, a pamphlet or brochure is a great way to further highlight your services to clients and other organizations. Your typical tri-fold pamphlet allows six separate surfaces for describing your selling points. For example, commercial business, residential business, unique selling points, reasons why your service is the best, who you are, and how to get in touch with you.

// You can design it yourself or hire a professional to design it. Get a second opinion if you decide to do it yourself. The last thing you want is to spend a lot of money printing a thousand pamphlets with a weak design, misspelled words or inaccurate information.

// Remember that advertising can make or break your credibility and secure or lose you new business. Pictures say a thousand words. Consider using 'before' and 'after' shots of your best work or include a recent headshot of yourself so that clients can put a face to the name. In addition to your website, a pamphlet is a great visual tool – make it as illustrative as possible.

Distributing doorknob hangers

// Hangers can be an immediate and cost effective way of spreading the good word about your new auctioneering service. First decide how much you are willing to spend on a thousand hanging flyers – and remember that black and white is cheaper than color printing. Count on spending anywhere from $50 to $150 per thousand doorknob hanging flyers. Once in hand, take the flyers to the most affluent neighborhoods in your area (keeping in mind any no-soliciting signs or laws which may exist).

Cultivating commercial and military business

// Your biggest and most profitable jobs will come from commercial businesses, especially ones with multiple locations. Securing big business may only require 'soft' selling but it's a good idea to call the location and ask for the property manager to BID on your business. A manager who can look like a hero by saving the company money will welcome a quote from you to compare with his/her current auctioneer. If you're asking more than the current provider, offer to underbid or provide an incentive – for instance, 20% off the price of the first job.

// One commercial contract can financially set up your business for the year for two reasons—multiple location/branches and repeat business. Remember the 80/20 rule - 80% of your business will come from 20% of your customers. Banks, for example, can become your bread and butter because of high foreclosure rates. Imagine auctioning off the reclaimed assets or properties of ten or more banks a year (in addition to your other jobs). It's guaranteed income for your business.

// Military bases outsource all service jobs! If you live near a base, call and request the necessary application forms to bid on upcoming contracts. Ask the base to put you on a mailing list for notification of future projects. If your writing skills aren't great, pay someone to set up a tender template for you and use this template every time you apply for a job. Check this website for more information on what is required to lodge a tender application with the military: www.ccr.gov.

// Once you gain access to the base, you should look at ways of capturing a fairly isolated market - the servicemen and women stationed at the base. Since most of these people are not local and may be living 'on site' temporarily, they seldom know who to use or trust when it comes to meeting their business needs. Speak to the people you meet and hand out lots of your business cards. Offer discounts to these folks whenever possible.

Giving away freebies and supporting charity organizations

// Give and you shall receive! This might not sound like a cost-effective way of advertising your services, but offering freebies now and then is a valuable way of connecting with your local community. It also makes for great publicity! When getting started, charity auctions give you a chance to gain experience and practice your craft. Unless you've had previous exposure to the industry, you'll need to become visible and well known in your area. You are under no pressure to perform jobs for free – but your clients won't forget you if you do! The more hours you've worked on big jobs, the quicker and easier it will become to devote a couple of hours to a free gig once in a while.

// Do you belong to a sporting club or church? Offer to host a couple of free auctions a year for any charitable or non profit organization you are involved in. Ask if they will give you exposure by mentioning you in a newsletter or bulletin. Churches and other places of worship have a strong following among parishioners and will most likely give you an honorable mention in their weekly publication if you have helped them out. Schools often hold fundraising events as well. Ask your friends or neighbors for ideas about who to get in touch with.

// Instead of holding a garage sale at your friends' or neighbors' homes, host an auction. Your friends will refer you to people they know and this time you can charge them a reduced rate and make some money. You'll be amazed by how many times you can receive referral business from committing to just one event. The greater your effort, the better the return.

// Distribute seasonal gift baskets to VIP clients – businesses who have offered you repeat referrals or customers who have remained loyal for a long time. These "marketing tools" don't have to be fancy - go to the dollar store, purchase a simple wicker basket and pick out some candy, cookies, stuffed toys, a pot plant or some fresh fruit. Drop these baskets off with tons of business cards and any other promotional material about your service. With any luck, you'll make some new friends, pick up additional business and receive a gift or two in return!

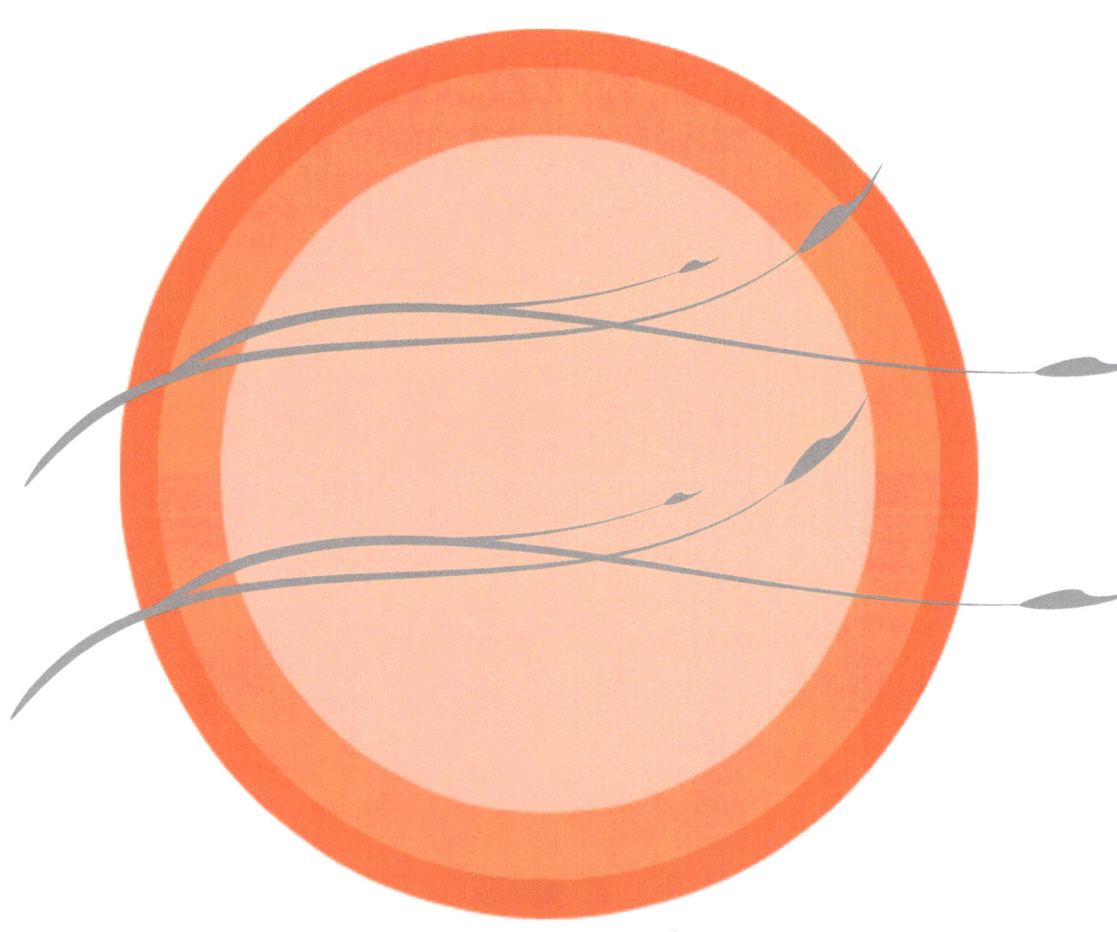

We hope you are excited and ready to get started with your new business venture!

There is so much commercial and residential business to be had – and it's up to you to go after it.

So don't delay -
start making great money today!

We'd love to hear from you!
Send your success stories to: businessguides@live.com

Resource Guide

US Small Business Administration

409 3rd Street, SW
Washington, DC 20416
SBA Answer Desk
1-800-U-ASK-SBA (1-800-827-5722)
Send e-mails to: answerdesk@sba.gov
Answer Desk TTY: (704) 344-6640
www.sba.gov

U.S. Chamber of Commerce

1615 H Street, NW
Washington, DC 20062-2000
Main Number: 202-659-6000
Customer Service: 1-800-638-6582
1615 H St NW Washington DC 20062
www.chamberofcommerce.com

Better Business Bureau

4200 Wilson Blvd, Suite 800
Arlington, VA 22203-1838
Phone: 1 (703) 276.0100
Fax: 1 (703) 525.8277
www.bbb.org

www.ingramcontent.com/pod-product-compliance
Lightning Source LLC
Chambersburg PA
CBHW050424180526
45159CB00005B/2403